GREAT
WINTER
OLYMPIC
MOMENTS

GREAT
WINTER
OLYMPIC
MOMENTS

Nate Aaseng

Lerner Publications Company
Minneapolis

Page 1: Veikko Hakulinen took Finland's cross-country ski relay team to victory at Squaw Valley, California, in 1960.

Page 2: Ski jumper Matti "Nukes" Nykänen shoots down the takeoff ramp at over 55 miles an hour.

Library of Congress Cataloging-in-Publication Data

Aaseng, Nathan.
   Great Winter Olympic moments / Nate Aaseng.
     p.   cm.
   Summary: Describes thirteen great victories and achievements during the Winter Olympic Games as athletes made history with their record-breaking performances.
   ISBN 0-8225-1535-0 (lib. bdg.)
   1. Winter Olympics—History—Juvenile literature. 2. Athletes—Biography—Juvenile literature. [1. Winter Olympics—History. 2. Athletes.] I. Title.
GV841.5.A18   1990   89-28752
796.98—dc20   CIP
                                 AC

Manufactured in the United States of America

1 2 3 4 5 6 7 8 9 10 99 98 97 96 95 94 93 92 91 90

Contents

After archaeologists discovered the ruins of the ancient Stadium of Olympia in Greece, Baron Pierre de Coubertin set out to revive the Olympic Games.

Introduction

Olympic founder Baron Pierre de Coubertin worked hard to make his dream of a modern Olympic competition come true. He spent several years drumming up support and finding financial backers for his project. De Coubertin's hard work paid off in 1896, when the first modern Games were held in Greece, home of the ancient Olympiad. The 1896 Olympic Games, which included only warm-weather sports, were a huge success. The idea of a Winter Olympics, on the other hand, was not nearly as well received. Olympic officials actually did their best to prevent the Winter Olympics from coming about!

Winter sports made their first Olympic appearance in 1908. The host country for that year, Great Britain, added several figure skating events to the regular Olympic program of track and field, wrestling, and swimming. Sweden declined to include any cold-weather sports in its 1912 Olympic program. But in the following Olympics (which were postponed until 1920, due to World War I), the host

Belgians included both figure skating and the relatively unknown sport of ice hockey.

This offered encouragement to fans of other winter sports, who wished for their sports to be included in the Olympics. The International Olympic Committee (IOC), however, refused to allow anyone to tamper with its Olympic dream. There was to be only one Olympics, the IOC declared, which would be held in the summer.

France, however, was more sympathetic to the winter sports enthusiasts. The French had never liked the idea of cramming all the Olympic events into a few weeks. When France had first hosted the Olympics back in 1900, the competition had been a loosely run series of events stretching over a three-month period. When the French were chosen to host the 1924 Games, they saw no reason not to tack on some winter competition early in the year. Skiers, skaters, bobsledders, and hockey teams were invited to Chamonix, France, to

Thousands of spectators flocked to Athens for the 1896 Games. The modern Olympics had begun.

participate in a special competition during the winter of 1924. This competition was so enthusiastically received that the International Olympic Committee had a change of heart. On May 27, 1925, the IOC voted to endorse a separate Winter Olympics. In fact, they declared the Chamonix competiton, which had been held without their backing, to be the first official Winter Olympic Games.

The IOC granted the host country of the Summer Olympics the option of also hosting the Winter Olympics. The Netherlands, which was hosting the next Summer Olympics, did not have facilities for a full range of winter sports. As a result, the 1928 Winter Games were awarded to Switzerland and were held in St. Moritz. Germany was the only country to take advantage of the option to hold both Olympics; it did so in 1936. Eventually, sites for the Winter and Summer Olympics came to be awarded separately.

The first Winter Olympics included bobsledding, ski jumping, ice hockey, figure skating, speed skating, and cross-country skiing. Over the years, Alpine skiing, ice dancing, luge, and other

The International Olympic Committee opposed the Winter Games, but that didn't stop the ski jumpers from flying at Chamonix in 1924.

events have been added to the program. The total number of participants has risen from fewer than 300 in 1924 to more than 1,300 in 1988. While growing into a major international sporting event, the Winter Olympic Games have provided a stage for many of the finest athletes ever to perform on ice and snow. This book captures some of the most thrilling moments of Winter Olympic competition.

Sonja Henie embellished her performances with spins, jumps, and dance moves.

1

The Child Champion

Sonja Henie
1936

In the women's figure skating competition at the 1924 Olympics, Sonja Henie fell during the free-skating program, and she finished dead last in the overall scoring. Such a performance was not surprising. After all, Henie was only 11 years old at the time.

Even in defeat, though, Henie had served notice of what was to come. Despite her fall and her inexperience, the tiny young Norwegian had placed third in the free-skating program—the portion of the competition in which skaters arrange their own routines. When Henie returned to Olympic competition four years later, she did not fall. She did not finish last. She took first place by a wide margin! By age 15, the remarkable Norwegian already displayed such creativity and precision that she had entirely changed the sport of figure skating.

Sonja Henie was born in 1912 to a wealthy Norwegian couple. When she was just a toddler, she saw an ice carnival in Switzerland. Sonja was so excited by the performance that she declared that she wanted to be an ice queen. Her parents started her off with ballet lessons at age four and gave her ice skates at age five. By the time she was eight years old, Sonja was winning amateur skating competitions.

With her father, a former cycling champion, as her coach, Henie learned the basics well. She mastered her "school figures" for the compulsory portion of the competition in which skaters are graded on their ability to trace precise figures marked on the ice. But she showed special skill in developing her free-skating program, the more colorful portion of the competition in which skaters are evaluated on

Under the watchful eyes of the judges, Henie methodically traces figures onto the ice.

their own arrangement of jumps and spins.

By age nine, Sonja was Norway's national women's skating champion. She showed unusual determination for one so young. It was not out of the ordinary for Sonja to practice seven hours a day. Her efforts paid off. At the age of 14, she captured her first World Championship title.

When Henie earned her first title, figure skating was not a popular sport, nor did it involve the sophisticated jumps and spins required of modern skaters. The freestyle, or free-skating, competition involved waltzing around the ice with a few simple turns and jumps added for good measure. Henie was a natural athlete (at one time she was considered the third-best female tennis player in her country), so she was easily able to master the basics.

But it was Henie's introduction of a new style of skating that made her unbeatable. After watching a performance by ballet star Anna Pavlova in the summer of 1927, Henie began experimenting with ballet moves on the ice. She later said that her advantage over her competitors was that she was too young to realize that she was not supposed to dance on the ice. During her career, Henie developed more than a dozen different types of spins and jumps. The grace and beauty of the ballet moves not only helped Henie in competition

but also attracted many new fans to her sport.

Henie easily captured the gold medal in women's figure skating at the 1928 Olympics in St. Moritz. The rave reviews she received for her performances catapulted her into international stardom. People who would not have crossed the street to watch figure skating a few years earlier packed auditoriums by the thousands to watch Henie perform.

When Henie arrived in Lake Placid, New York, to defend her Olympic title in 1932, the crowds clogged the stairways of the auditorium for more than an hour before her appearance. That year the women's figure skating event could hardly be called a competition. In the eyes of most spectators, it was the Sonja Henie Show. Deafening applause greeted Henie as she glided onto the ice, and the audience never stopped cheering and clapping all through her performance. Henie captured the gold medal by a huge margin.

While Henie's performances delighted Olympic audiences in 1928 and 1932, her most dramatic effort came in her final Olympic appearance. After reigning as the women's world champion for 10

Inspired by Henie's performances, young skaters like Cecilia Colledge brought a new competitive spirit to figure skating.

competition, and she wanted to go out a winner.

This time, however, victory was not guaranteed. Inspired by Henie's success over the past decade, a new generation of skaters had risen to challenge her. In the European championships earlier that year, the judges had actually given the highest score in the free-skating program to 15-year-old Cecilia Colledge of Great Britain. Only Henie's slight advantage in the compulsory school figures had allowed her to hold on to her championship.

In the 1936 Olympics at Garmisch-Partenkirchen, Germany, Henie lost most of that edge. After the compulsory figures, Henie held only a 3.6-point lead over her taller, younger opponent. Colledge then put more pressure on with a stunning free-skating performance. Even though she almost fell once, Colledge earned high marks.

Henie would have to come up with her best performance in many years to beat her teenage rival. With 11,000 fans applauding her every move, the champion glided and whirled around the ice with cool determination. As she finished with a graceful double jump, ending in

consecutive years, the 24-year-old Henie was ready to turn professional. The 1936 Olympics were to be her final amateur

Ex-skating champion Arthur Vieregg congratulates Henie after her Olympic victory in 1936.

the splits, the audience roared its approval. The judges agreed and gave Henie an even higher score than they had given Colledge.

The woman who has been described as having "brought figure skating to the world" could not have scripted a more fitting finish to her Olympic career.

Andrea Mead Lawrence just wanted to have fun on the slopes. Along the way, she won an Olympic gold medal.

2

Down But Not Out

Andrea Mead Lawrence
1952

Alpine skiers (downhill and slalom racers) are gamblers by nature. They calculate how fast they can go or how tightly they can take a turn without any risk of falling, then they push their luck. They take the turn faster or cut it more closely than they should and trust to their luck to pull them through. Andrea Mead Lawrence was a champion skier who lost one such gamble at a crucial time. In a race where a slight slip can cost a racer a medal, Lawrence lost her balance completely and fell. But that error turned out to be a blessing rather than a disaster. If she had not fallen, Lawrence would still have been remembered as one of the United States' finest skiers. But by falling, she set the stage for Olympic stardom.

Andrea Mead was born in Rutland, Vermont, in 1932. Her parents traveled to Switzerland to ski every year, and they eventually set up their own ski resort at home. Andy began gliding down the slopes in her backyard at the age of four. At first she learned simply by watching her parents, but later she received private instruction from a pro.

Andy made the United States Olympic ski team in 1948. The 15-year-old did poorly in the fast downhill race, in which skiers hurtle at top speeds over a long course that has only a few turn markers or "gates" in it. But she came closer to a medal in the slalom event. In this race, in which skiers must zigzag through a series of closely spaced gates, Mead took an eighth-place finish.

Over the next couple of years, Mead's interest in the sport that had consumed much of her life began to fade. She nearly gave up skiing in 1949 and suffered through a poor racing season the following year. Finally, a United States

17

ski team coach persuaded Mead to spend a year away from competition. During her time off, Mead rediscovered the sheer pleasure of skiing. From then on, she was determined that she would not get caught up in the pressure of winning or losing. She raced just for the fun of it; whether she won or lost did not matter so much. Andy even bristled if her new husband, skier Dave Lawrence, wished her luck in a race. She asked him just to remind her to have fun instead.

Andy soon found that fun and success could go hand in hand. She easily made the Olympic team in 1952 and was even considered one of the favorites. She quickly lived up to expectations in the Oslo, Norway, Olympics by winning the giant slalom, a race that is similar to the regular slalom, but held on a longer course with more widely spaced gates. In this race, Andy defeated Austrian film star Dagmar Rom by more than two seconds. As usual, the downhill race was more difficult for Lawrence than were the slalom runs. Lawrence fell twice during her run and finished 17th.

That left only the regular slalom event. But a shortage of snow caused problems. Some of the snow that had been brought in by the Norwegian army had melted and become icy. Officials were afraid that this would increase the racers' speeds so much that they might risk serious injury. In an effort to slow the skiers down, officials planted extra gates on the course. With 49 turns on the 508-yard (457-meter) course, skiers would be spending more time turning and going back and forth across the mountain and less time going down it at breakneck speeds.

Gretchen Fraser, manager of the U.S. women's ski team, helps Lawrence prepare for Olympic competition.

The icy course at Oslo couldn't dampen Andy's spirits.

While these changes bothered some skiers, Lawrence shrugged them off. Since her change of heart in 1950, she had rarely felt nervous before a race. She was just there to have fun; it didn't matter what the course was like. In the first round or "heat" of the two-heat event, Lawrence fearlessly charged down the hill. While still on the flatter, top portion of the course, Lawrence tried to cut some time with a dangerous jump. She skidded across the ice and caught the tip of a ski on a course marker. Lawrence slid sideways into a pile of snow and fell on her hip. As she later said, "I made a great jump—right off the course!"

With that, Lawrence's hopes for another medal seemed to be dashed. Had she been more intent on winning instead of having fun, the shock of the fall might have ended her run. Instead, Lawrence simply bounced to her feet, sidestepped up the hill a short way to get back on course, and resumed her run.

She took even more chances during the rest of the run. She flew across the finish line with a time of one minute, seven and two-tenths seconds (1:07.2).

Lawrence's fall cost her four seconds, but it didn't keep her from coming up with the best combined time in the women's slalom at Oslo.

Those who had seen her fall were baffled when the finishing time was announced. They estimated that Lawrence's fall cost her four seconds. Yet she made up enough time in the lower part of the course to finish with the fourth-best time of the day! The leader, Ossi Reichert of Germany, had beaten her by only 1.2 seconds!

Despite the treacherous course (Dagmar Rom had also fallen and was disqualified from the competition),

Lawrence was as determined as ever to have some fun on her second run. She took just as many chances as ever, but this time she won all her gambles. Lawrence flashed down the course in a time of 1:03.4, a full two seconds faster than her closest competitor.

Her sizzling second run gave her the fastest combined time for the two runs. Because of her poise and her daring, Andrea Mead Lawrence turned disaster into a gold medal.

No one could touch Toni Sailer at the Cortina d'Ampezzo Olympics. In the giant slalom, the second-fastest skier finished more than six seconds behind him.

3

King of the Hill

Toni Sailer
1956

Austrian skier Andreas Molterer was the favorite in the 1956 Olympic giant slalom race in Cortina d'Ampezzo, Italy. Molterer sped down the strenuous, 1.7-mile (2.7-kilometer) ski course in nearly flawless fashion. His time of 3:06.3 easily beat all of those who had come down the hill before him.

Spectators congratulated Molterer and assured him that after such a run, the gold medal was certainly his. Molterer, however, put a stop to the victory celebration with a single, short sentence: "Toni hasn't come yet."

Molterer was talking about his teammate, Anton "Toni" Sailer. He knew that it did not matter how he skied against anyone else in the 1956 Olympics. To win the gold medal, Molterer had to withstand the charge of the greatest skier in the world.

Anton Sailer was born in 1935 and grew up in the Austrian Alps, in the community of Kitzbühel. Toni got his first pair of skis a couple of weeks before his second birthday. Toni enjoyed plenty of other sports besides skiing as a boy. He did well at tennis, soccer, and swimming. Only when his sister began dating a champion Austrian skier did Toni begin to concentrate on skiing. He improved rapidly, and at the age of 16 he was among those battling for a spot on the 1952 Austrian Olympic team. That dream came to an abrupt end when Toni broke his leg during training.

Sailer recovered from his injury and continued his ski career while working as a plumber. By the time of the 1956 Olympics, Sailer had demonstrated exceptional ability and had made the Austrian team. Coaches marveled at the way Toni could keep his skis flat on the snow, even over rutted sections,

Sailer easily took medals in the slalom and the giant slalom. But the faster downhill event was his favorite.

and how he could make split-second decisions at high speeds. It seemed that Sailer never made a mistake.

Sailer was at a loss to explain his skiing style. One opponent, awed by Sailer's flawless performances, thought he knew the answer. He declared that Toni was able to feel the snow through his skis.

For a while, though, it looked as if Sailer might have to sit out yet another Olympics. As has often happened in Olympic history, the weather did not cooperate. Cortina d'Ampezzo, the Winter Olympic site, experienced one of its driest winters in years, and the slopes were almost bare in the weeks preceding the Games. A 14-inch (35-centimeter) snowstorm arrived just in time. But the storm was followed by a thaw and a freeze, which left the mountains glazed with treacherous ice.

Ice was not the only threat to Andreas Molterer and the other skiers, however. As Sailer came down the giant slalom course, Molterer realized that his own time could not hold up against his teammate's effort. Carving perfect arcs through the turns, Sailer finished the giant slalom in a time of 3:00.1—more than six seconds faster than Molterer! His first gold medal could hardly have come more easily.

From there it was on to the shorter slalom event, which would be run on two different courses. Because of the ice and the tight turns, many experts thought the two slalom courses were the most difficult they had ever seen. Sailer recorded the fastest time on both of the slalom runs. In a race that is often decided by fractions of a second, Sailer defeated second-place Chiharu Igaya of Japan by four seconds for his second gold medal.

The most difficult and dangerous test —the downhill—remained. The course had been named after a local racer who was killed while skiing it. The run sent competitors hurtling alongside bare cliffs and rocky crags. A sheet of ice covered much of the course, and strong winds whipped around the mountain. Only 17 out of 75 skiers came through the course without falling or missing gates.

Sailer was nearly done in before the race even started. As he tightened his boot straps before his run, one of them snapped. The Austrian team was caught completely off guard. None of them had a spare strap. Fortunately, a trainer on the Italian team offered Toni a strap from his own binding.

Despite this unnerving start, the pressure of going for a third Alpine title in one Olympics, and the fact that many expert skiers were crashing, Sailer appeared eager for the race. He preferred the downhill race to the slaloms, he said, because he "didn't have to brake so much." Smiling and wearing a bright yellow scarf, Toni blasted off from the starting line.

His reckless enthusiasm nearly cost him the race. Early in the course, Sailer hit a bump and flew into the air, dangerously off balance. By the time he landed, though, he was back in control. Sailer zoomed through the rest of the course without a problem. Again his margin of victory was astounding. Silver-medal-winner Raymond Fellay of Switzerland finished 3.5 seconds behind.

While Toni Sailer is not the only skier to have won all three events in an Olympic Alpine skiing contest, he dominated his races in a way that is unlikely to be matched in any Olympic competition.

Cross-country skiing was an obscure sport in 1960 when Väinö Huhtala and his Finnish teammates came to Squaw Valley, California.

4

Marathon Photo Finish

The 4 x 10 Cross-Country Relay
1960

In contrast to the breakneck speeds and the brushes with disaster typical of Alpine skiing, cross-country skiing often seems like a stroll in the park—a pleasant, peaceful exercise.

Except in the northern European countries and the Soviet Union, cross-country skiers have been largely ignored. They kick and glide along trails for hours, undisturbed by television cameras. The cross-country relay race is the only Winter Olympic event in which athletes race against each other instead of against a clock. As a result, this race has more potential for exciting finishes than any other event. This was shown in 1960, when cross-country skiers from Finland and Norway put on a battle of wills that left the spectators nearly as exhausted as the competitors.

The 1960 Olympics were held in Squaw Valley, California. There were not many cross-country skiers in the United States at that time and there was little spectator interest in the cross-country events being held at McKinney Creek in Squaw Valley. Those fans who did turn out were prepared to settle in for a long wait: the skiers competed at distances of up to 50 kilometers (30 miles). In every cross-country race except the relay, skiers leave at 30-second intervals and race against the clock. It is often difficult to tell who is leading until the race is over.

In the 4 x 10-kilometer relay, however, all competitors in the first leg start out together. Four racers from each team cover 10 kilometers (6 miles) apiece, for a total distance roughly equal to that of a marathon foot race. Norway and Finland were the relay favorites, with Sweden and the Soviet Union also rated as contenders.

As the first racers completed their leg of the course, Lars Olsson of Sweden led the pack. Following close on his heels were racers from Norway, Finland, and the Soviet Union. There is no baton exchange in a cross-country ski relay; team members simply tag the next racer when they complete their leg of the race. With Janne Stefansson taking over from Olsson, Sweden seemed in good shape. After all, Stefansson had finished seventh in the 15-kilometer race.

Finland, however, had put Eero Mäntyranta into the second slot. Mäntyranta, a young border guard who earned his living by patrolling on skis, had finished sixth in the 15 kilometers. Norway had countered with Hallgeir Brenden, a gold-medal winner in the 1952 and 1956 games. With surprising ease, both Mäntyranta and Brenden quickly passed Stefansson.

When the Norwegian Brenden glided into the finish area even with Mäntyranta at the end of the second leg, Norway appeared to be on its way to victory. It had saved two fine skiers for the last two legs. Einar Östby, who had just missed a bronze medal in the 15-kilometer race, took over the third leg.

Hakon Brusveen, the 15-kilometer gold medalist, was waiting to ski the final 10 kilometers.

As expected, Östby cruised into the lead and gradually drew away. Sweden fell far off the pace, which meant that the Norwegians would not have to worry about the great Sixten Jernberg, who was racing the final leg for the Swedes. At the end of the third leg, the only skier within sight of Norway's Östby was Finland's Väinö Huhtala.

Norway's Hakon Brusveen sped off, holding a 200-yard (180-m) lead over the Finnish team. Behind him, a 35-year-old lumberjack was skimming swiftly along the ski trail. Veikko Hakulinen, a six-time Olympic medalist, had not been enjoying the 1960 Olympics. The Finn had used the wrong wax on his skis and had failed miserably in his specialty, the 30-kilometer race. Now he stalked Brusveen, determined to redeem himself. Slowly, he began to cut into the Norwegian's big lead.

Hakulinen inched closer and closer. On the last long uphill portion of the race, he closed to within striking distance. With one and a quarter miles (2 km) to go, Hakulinen passed his rival.

Hakulinen charges toward the finish line with Brusveen less than a second behind.

Brusveen refused to concede. For the next mile, he stayed right on the heels of the Finn. With 200 yards (180 m) to go, the Norwegian began his final spurt to pass Hakulinen. Brusveen came up beside Hakulinen's shoulder, fighting with the last of his strength. Spectators looked on in anguish as the two neared the finish line.

But as Brusveen remarked after the race, "That fella just refused to get tired." Hakulinen held off Brusveen in the final charge and crossed the finish line three feet (1 m) in front of him.

Overcome with emotion, the Finns carried Hakulinen from the grounds on their shoulders. Incredibly, after 40 kilometers (24 miles) of racing, only .8 seconds had separated the Finns from the Norwegians!

Lydia Skoblikova blazes her way to another speed skating victory.

5

One-Woman Gold Rush

Lydia Skoblikova
1964

There was no doubt that Soviet speed skater Lydia Skoblikova would return from the 1964 Olympics in Innsbruck, Austria, wearing gold. The only question was how much.

Lydia Skoblikova already owned two Olympic gold medals going into the 1964 Games. In 1960 she had won the 3,000 meters and had set a world record in capturing the 1,500 meters. She had also just missed a bronze medal in the 1,000 meters. Since then, the schoolteacher from Chelyabinsk, a town in Siberia, had shown championship form in the sprints as well as in the longer distances. She had won all four of the women's races at the 1963 World Championships.

In Innsbruck, however, the 24-year-old Skoblikova did not plan to enter the 500 meters. Her main competition in that race would be her own teammates. Skoblikova worried that she would be considered greedy if she deprived them of a possible gold medal when she already was assured of so many. Others, however, encouraged Lydia to give her best effort in all the races. Among these was her husband back home, who sent a message urging her to "win as many as you can." In the end, these arguments won out.

Skoblikova expected the first speed skating event, the 500 meters, to be her toughest race. Unfortunately, as she was racing, she would have no way to judge just how stiff the competition was. Ever since a disastrous attempt in 1932 to have all skaters compete against each other in a single race, Olympic speed skating has been a battle against the clock. Skaters now race in pairs around an oval track. When all the heats have been run, the order of the finish is determined by comparing individual

By the end of the 1964 Games, Skoblikova had added four more gold medals to her collection.

times. Lydia had to skate her best race and hope that her time held up against the competition.

Her best race turned out to be an Olympic record. As expected, Skoblikova's Soviet teammates were the closest competitors, but none of them could match her time of 45.0 seconds. With a gold medal in her weakest race, Lydia was expected to easily capture the other three.

There was little suspense as Lydia cruised through two and a half laps of the 400-meter (440-yard) rink in the 1,000 meter race. By this time, the crowd had grown to appreciate her grace and power as she smoothly swung her arm in clock-like rhythm and cross-stepped neatly around the difficult turns. They urged her on as she chased after another Olympic record. Long after the race was over, the spectators cheered wildly. The noise was so great that Skoblikova's Olympic record time of 1:33.2 had to be announced five times before anyone could hear it.

Skoblikova's margin of victory in this race was a little narrower than usual—just over one second. But she thrilled the crowd with a more convincing performance in the 1,500 meters. Her Olympic-record time of 2:22.6 defeated Finland's Kaija Mustonen by nearly three seconds.

It was the final race, the 3,000 meters, that posed the most strenuous challenge. Not only was it the longest of her four races, but it would be her fourth race in as many days. To make matters worse, the Winter Olympics had been cursed with mild weather. Innsbruck's warmest winter in nearly 60 years threatened to put a halt to Skoblikova's run of gold medals. By luck of the draw, Lydia's teammate, Valentina Stenina, raced in one of the earlier heats. Stenina's time of 5:18.5 was not particularly fast for the distance. But as the temperature rose, and the ice began to soften and melt, it seemed quite possible that no one could beat it.

There was no need to worry. Skating in the seventh heat, Skoblikova went out at a steady pace. Midway through the race, her coaches, checking their stopwatches, informed her that she was one second ahead of Stenina's time. But the pace was much slower than she was used to. So Lydia instinctively began to speed up. Soviet coaches pleaded with her to save her strength, and she backed off. Near the end of the race, with all spectators eyeing the clock, the champion began her final surge. With powerful strides and with her arms flying out from one side to the other, she blazed to the finish line.

Her time of 5:14.9 was actually slower than her time of four years before. But on the soft ice, it was an incredible achievement. Most importantly, it was fast enough to take over first place.

One more challenge remained. As Skoblikova was being congratulated for her effort, an unknown North Korean was taking her turn on the ice. As the crowd watched in amazement, tiny Pil-Hwa Han matched Skoblikova's pace, stride for stride, around the soggy track. Moved by the North Korean's determined effort, the crowd began to urge her on. After four of the seven laps, Pil-Hwa Han was still even with the pace of the great champion. With one lap to go, she was only one second behind. Her valiant effort, however, could not overcome Skoblikova's finishing kick. Lydia Skoblikova had survived a final scare to earn a record four gold medals in a single Winter Olympics.

The Italian bobsled team, led by Eugenio Monti (far right) took a silver medal at Cortina d'Ampezzo. But Monti wouldn't let up in his quest for gold.

6

Gold at the End of the Tunnel

Eugenio Monti
1968

If there were a Hall of Fame for bob-sledders, one entire wing could easily to be dedicated to Eugenio Monti. Monti dominated his sport for more than a decade. Other bobsledders referred to Monti as "the master."

The native of Cortina d'Ampezzo, Italy, began his sports career as an Alpine skier. He was considered one of Italy's best. Then in 1952, he suffered a horrible fall in which he tore ligaments in both knees. Doctors told him that he would never be able to ski competitively again.

For a time, Monti turned his attention to sports car racing. Two years later, though, he discovered a way to combine his driving skill with his love of winter sports. In 1954 Monti began competing as a bobsledder. In bobsledding, teams of two or four contestants ride a sled down a long, winding chute. The team with the fastest combined time after four runs wins the competition.

The driver, or front rider, is the most important member of the bobsledding team. Back riders help the driver by providing a starting push, leaning into the turns, and keeping low on the sled to cut down on wind resistance. But the driver is responsible for steering a straight line along the course, keeping control of the sled in the turns, and keeping the sled from bumping the walls of the chute. In a sport in which more weight on the sled creates more speed, the 145-pound (65-kilogram) Monti was at a disadvantage. But he learned the techniques of driving so well that, within two years, he was a strong challenger for an Olympic gold medal.

In the 1956 Olympics, held in Monti's hometown, the little Italian came close to winning the gold medal he so badly wanted. He finished second to another Italian team in the two-man bobsled competition and took second to a Swiss team in the four-man event.

Monti was probably at his peak at the time of the 1960 Olympics. He was in the middle of a streak of five straight World Championship titles in the two-man bobsled. Unfortunately, the Squaw Valley, California, site had no bobsled run. Monti had to wait until the 1964 games in Innsbruck, Austria, before he could get another shot at the gold.

After two runs of the two-man bobsled at the Innsbruck Games, the British team of Anthony Nash and Robin Dixon had taken the lead. But as the two were preparing for their third run, they discovered that a bolt supporting one of their sled runners had broken. With their sled disabled, Nash and Dixon would have to drop out of the competition.

When Monti heard of the British team's problem, he did not hesitate. He removed a bolt from his own sled and gave it to the British. With their sled now back in the competition, Nash and Dixon continued to hold the lead after three rounds. Monti trailed by .23 seconds going into the last round.

The British made their final run and were disappointed with their time. They were certain that Monti would beat it. By the time Monti came down, though, the ice on the course had softened and was not as slippery as before. Monti could do no better than third place. Although he was disappointed, he refused to blame the course conditions. He congratulated the British and told the press that he had driven poorly.

Further disappointment awaited Monti in the four-man competition. This time it was a Canadian team that rocketed to victory, while Monti and his teammates finished third. The Canadians made a point of thanking Monti for teaching them the finer points of bobsledding. But it was still humiliating for the old master to be beaten by Canada, a country that did not have a single bobsled run. At the end of the 1964 Games, Monti was ready to admit defeat. He declared that he was retiring from bobsledding.

Four years later, though, Monti was back looking for gold at the 1968 Games. Few people thought the 40-year-old had much of a chance. In the past few years, Erwin Thaler of Austria had

Bobsled racing is a dangerous sport. Monti (front) had been battered in numerous crashes, and his face was badly scarred.

proven himself to be the best bobsled driver in the world.

Monti studied the Olympic course in Grenoble, France, with great care. When it was his turn to compete in the two-man bobsled, Monti was ready. After three trips down the mountain, Monti found his team trailing the leaders by only .1 seconds. So close to his dream, Monti drove his final run with grim determination. Whipping through the turns with precision, the sled came through with a course-record time of 1:10.05.

Now all Monti could do was watch as Horst Floth of West Germany sped down the chute. Floth and his teammate drove a remarkable race. Their time of 1:10.15 left them tied with Monti, with a total time for the four heats of 4:41:54. According to international bobsled racing rules, in case of a tie, victory goes to the sled recording the single fastest run—that was Monti's record-setting 1:10.05. Monti nearly collapsed with relief. His 12-year quest for gold had finally paid off. "Now I can retire a happy man," he sighed.

Monti then drove a four-man sled to a .11-second victory over the favored Austrians to pick up a second gold medal. Erwin Thaler then paid Monti a fitting final tribute. "If we must lose," he said, "we're glad it's to Monti."

On the slopes and off, flashy Jean-Claude Killy was the center of attention at the Grenoble Games.

7

The French Superstar

Jean-Claude Killy
1968

Jean-Claude Killy was the James Bond of Alpine skiing. Totally fearless in the face of danger, Killy skied not only with skill but also with a dashing style all his own. Whether engaged in intense competition or surrounded by hordes of admirers, the ruggedly handsome Frenchman always seemed in complete control.

Killy dominated the 1968 Winter Olympics as no athlete had done before. In those Grenoble Games, however, Killy very nearly became a victim of his own popularity. Even Toni Sailer had not been the favorite in every race when he won the three Alpine races in 1956. But Killy was *expected* to win all three.

Like many of the great European skiers, Killy grew up in a resort village in the Alps. He began skiing at the age of three in his home community of Val d'Isère, France. Killy was so committed

to the sport that he dropped out of school at 16 to join the French ski team.

A fine all-around skier, Killy qualified for the 1964 French Olympic team in all three Alpine events: downhill, slalom, and giant slalom. Killy's first Olympic performance was primarily a learning experience. Although he came close to a medal with a fifth-place finish in the slalom, he did not even finish the other two races.

By 1967, however, Killy had soared to the top in international skiing. During the 1966-67 season, he won 12 of 16 World Cup races, the most prestigious ski events on the international circuit. Adding to his dashing, invincible image, Killy won a sports car race the next summer.

Killy's style of racing was as impressive as his victories. He said that he cared nothing for technique, that everything was done on instinct, and that his only strategy was to go faster than he thought he could on every part of the course.

While Killy may not have planned it, he also developed a technique that intrigued ski experts. When coming out of a turn, Killy would sit back on his skis and thrust them forward. This gave him a little burst of power that could make the difference in a race in which tenths of a second are crucial.

Killy's success and popularity attracted many offers from ski manufacturers who wanted to pay the champion to promote their products. The Frenchman accepted some of these offers and nearly lost his amateur status and his chance to compete in the Olympics. It took some frantic negotiating by French authorities to keep their 24-year-old star eligible for the 1968 Games.

The first Alpine event in Grenoble, France, was the downhill. Killy's teammate, Guy Périllat, was first down the mountain. His sped through the nearly two-mile (3-km) course in under two minutes. None of the downhill experts from the other countries could match that mark. When he learned that Périllat was holding on to first place, Killy felt certain of victory. He began confidently, but slipped at the top of the course and dropped behind his teammate's pace. Halfway through the course, Killy had still not made up for his error.

Charging furiously through the final gates, Killy roared across the finish line just ahead of Périllat's time. Killy's hopes for a sweep of the Alpine events had survived by the scant margin of .08 seconds!

The giant slalom proved easier. Even though the contestants who skied before him had carved the course full of ruts, Killy beat out the next fastest skier by 1.2 seconds on the first run. A nearly identical second run gave him a victory of more than two seconds over Willy Favre of Switzerland. Killy was two-thirds of the way to his goal.

Before the slalom could begin, a thick fog began to blanket the mountain. Because it was difficult to see the flags that marked the course, skiers asked that the event be postponed. Officials, however, insisted on running the race as scheduled.

The sun shone on Killy that day, literally. As Killy, the first man on the

Some opponents charged that Killy should not have been allowed to compete in amateur competition.

course, charged down the slope, the sun broke through the fog. As soon as he finished, it disappeared again behind ever thicker clouds of fog. The Frenchman finished the first round with a narrow lead. But with 14 skiers bunched within one second of his leading time, the outcome was very much in doubt.

On his second run, Killy did well, but he did not appear invincible. A great

When the slalom contest ended, Karl Schranz (center) appeared to be the victor. Killy (right) and former champion Toni Sailer (left) offer their congratulations.

effort by one of Killy's rivals might be enough to beat him. By this time, the fog was so thick that many skiers were unable to see the flags and were disqualified for missing gates. U.S. skier Rich Chaffee summed up the situation when he explained his disqualification: "I made every gate I could see."

As each contestant took his run, hordes of Killy fans waited anxiously at the bottom of the hill, staring at the electronic clock. Austria's Herbert Huber had them holding their breath as he flashed across the finish line less than .1 seconds behind Killy's time. When Norway's Häkon Mjön skimmed across the finish line with a winning time, the Killy fans' hopes were dashed. Word quickly came down, however, that Mjön had missed two gates and had been disqualified. Karl Schranz of Austria then started down the course, only to be stopped by the sight of someone crossing the hill in front of him. After witnesses backed up Schranz's claim, the Austrian was awarded another run.

Schranz sliced through the gates flawlessly on his second run and snatched the victory from Killy. But a long argument began to rage. Two hours later, Schranz was disqualified after it was reported that he had missed two gates on his first run—before the interference had taken place. Austria then filed a protest with the Olympic officials.

By the narrowest of margins, a 3-2 vote, the Jury of Appeal turned down the protest. After a long wait, Jean-Claude Killy could finally relax. In one of the most chaotic finishes ever, Killy had joined Toni Sailer as the only Olympic skiers to sweep the Alpine events.

The Japanese team swept the 70-meter ski jump contest in Sapporo. At the awards ceremony, Konno, Kasaya, and Aochi wave to the hometown crowd.

8

Triumph of the Home Team

Yukio Kasaya
1972

Before 1972, Japanese athletes had won only one medal in Winter Olympic competition. In 1956 a skier named Chiharu Igaya had placed second to Toni Sailer in the slalom. Even that accomplishment had been tainted. Officials from two countries had protested Igaya's silver-medal run, claiming that he had missed a gate.

This lack of success weighed on the minds of many Japanese in 1972, because in that year, the Winter Olympics were to be held in Japan. The city of Sapporo, on Japan's northernmost island of Hokkaido, had been selected as the host site.

With their national pride at stake, the Japanese turned their eyes toward Yukio Kasaya. Most Olympic experts believed that if the host country had any chance to win a medal, it had to come from this slender ski jumper. Ski

jumping had traditionally been dominated by northern European athletes. But Kasaya had recently returned from Europe, where he had won three straight meets against the best competition he could find.

Traffic was heavy around Sapporo on February 6, 1972, as thousands of spectators made the trek to the mountain of Miyanomori. The grandstand seats at the bottom of the ski jump had been sold out for months. All three of the Japanese jumpers on the 70-meter hill were locals. As 28-year-old Yukio Kasaya, 27-year-old Akitsugu Konno, and 29-year-old Seiji Aochi climbed the steps of the ski jump, they could see the hillside overflowing with their neighbors and former classmates. During the practice jumps, the crowd marveled loudly at the leaps of the hometown favorites.

While masses of people milled around

45

the base of Miyanomori, Japan's normally bustling large cities were almost deserted. Those who were not at home watching the Games were crowded around televisions in store windows.

Such attention could have unnerved the three jumpers. As the first two rounds began, they steeled themselves against the pressure. Konno and Aochi shot into the air as if blasted out of a cannon and soared far down the hill. Spurred on by the crowd, each man leaned far over his skis and held the pose until the last possible instant. Konno and Aochi each landed more than 80 meters (88 yds) from the takeoff point—farther than any of the European jumpers had yet gone.

Now it was Kasaya's turn. He paused at the top of the jump tower to collect his thoughts. He could see, far away at the bottom of the hill, his old classmates waving the flag of Yoichimachi School. After positioning his skis in the tracks that dropped steeply down toward the end of the jump, Kasaya bowed his head and looked down the hill. He had been jumping on the hills near Sapporo since he was 11 years old, but this jump was far more important than the thousands of others he had made. After standing

motionless for more than a minute, Kasaya jumped onto the track.

At the end of the jumping platform, Kasaya launched himself high into the air and stretched his body ramrod straight over the skis. His flawless form carried him far down the hill—even farther than his two teammates had gone. As Kasaya's skis touched the snow, the crowd erupted in a deafening cheer. Although distance is the most important measure in ski jumping, judges may take points away from a jumper because of flaws in technique. Kasaya's graceful jumping style, added to his long distance, gave him the lead after the first round. Even more incredible, his teammates held second and third!

Now brimming with confidence, the three jumpers headed back up the hill for their second and final jumps. None of them could equal the distance of their first, emotion-inspired leaps. Kasaya's distance fell from 84 meters (92 yds) to 79 meters (87 yds). But it was still enough. When Kasaya planted his skis on the hill for a solid landing, he clasped his hands high over his head. No sooner had he stopped at the bottom of the hill than he was mobbed by

Kasaya flies to victory in the 70-meter jump.

teammates and coaches. He and his teammates had captured the gold, silver, and bronze medals.

Spectators were weeping, dancing, and leaping into the air. In all the years of Winter Olympic competition, Japan had gained just one medal. Now, performing in front of the home crowd, Japanese jumpers had taken three medals in a single event!

Franz Klammer, airborne above the downhill course at Innsbruck

9

Death-Defying Run

Franz Klammer
1976

As crushing as the pressure must have been on Killy and Kasaya, skier Franz Klammer, a farm boy from Mooswald, Austria, may have been carrying an even greater burden on his shoulders in the 1976 Olympics in Innsbruck, Austria.

Like Killy, Klammer was expected to win. After his record of eight wins in nine World Cup downhill races, anything less than an Olympic gold medal would be considered failure. Like Kasaya, Klammer was considered the host country's only real hope for a gold medal. In case Klammer did not understand the reality of this, Austrian officials provided a very public reminder. During the opening ceremonies, Klammer was chosen not only to carry the Austrian flag, but to take the Olympic oath on behalf of all athletes—pledging to observe proper sports etiquette. But there was more. Klammer knew that much of his

country's economy depended on him. Austria counted heavily on income from its winter tourist industry. A champion Olympic skier could provide Austria the priceless publicity that it needed to attract tourists.

In addition to these pressures from his home country, Klammer also had to contend with Bernhard Russi of Switzerland. Russi, the defending Olympic downhill champion, was at his best in important races. On the first day of serious competition in the 1976 Games, Russi posted a sizzling time of 1:46.06 over the 1.9-mile (3.1-km) downhill course.

At least the 22-year-old Klammer now knew exactly what he had to do. The great Austrian skier Karl Schranz once said that the downhill was a race that no coward would ever win. What Klammer was planning was certainly

Klammer (center) bested Bernhard Russi (right) at the World Cup races in Morzine, France. A month later, at the Innsbruck Olympics, Russi was again the man to beat.

not the strategy of a coward. If he was to have a chance at the the gold medal after Russi's remarkable run, Klammer would have to risk his own safety. It was a challenge that Franz was prepared to take.

Klammer was the last of the top-rated skiers to race. From his first burst out of the starting gate, it was obvious that Klammer meant business. In a dazzling gold uniform, he charged down the slope and careened through the turns. For the first quarter of the course, he skied perfectly. But he began to build up such incredible speed that several times he nearly lost control of his skis and came out of his racer's crouch position. This increased the wind resistance and slowed him down. By the halfway point, the Austrian star had fallen nearly .2 seconds behind Russi's pace.

If Klammer had appeared to be skiing recklessly on the top of the course, the middle part of his race was almost frightening. As the 70,000 spectators lining the slopes cringed, Franz plunged down steep banks and rattled over potholes and washboard bumps. Strength, athletic ability, and sheer determination kept him on his feet.

By the time he reached the bottom part of the course, Klammer had fallen even farther behind Russi's time. But he didn't let up. In most of his downhill victories, a strong finish had boosted Klammer past his rivals. As a boy living on a farm tucked high in the Alps, there had been little for Franz to do except work and ski. The skiing had helped him to develop skill, and the work had given him strength. Now, at a point where other racers began to tire from the exhausting effort, Klammer's strength came into play.

In the final 1,000 meters (1,100 yds), Klammer soared through a jump and then kept his balance through the dip that followed. Blazing down the slope at nearly 70 miles per hour (112 km/h), Franz dug his skis sharply into the snow. His powerful legs absorbed the strain, and he cut a sharper turn than had any of his rivals. Klammer nearly missed a gate and then roared over the final stretch of snow.

As he flashed by the finish line, the clock stopped at 1:45.73. Klammer had beaten Russi by just over .3 seconds. Some breathless spectators called his wild run for the gold the most frightening thing they had ever witnessed. But had Klammer only appeared to be flirting with danger? Had he really been in control? "I thought I was going to crash all the way," Franz confessed.

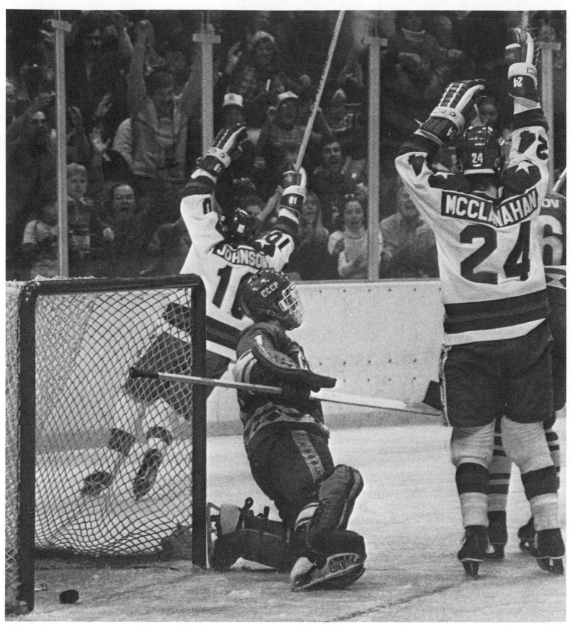

The Americans jump for joy. Mark Johnson's goal has just brought Team USA to a 3-3 tie with the Soviets. Victory is within reach.

10

The Miracle Machine

Team USA
1980

For 16 years, the Olympic hockey competition resembled feeding time at the lion's den. One team after another was served up to the invincible Soviet Union squad, which would methodically eat them up. Going into the 1980 Games in Lake Placid, New York, the Soviets had lost only 4 of their last 45 Olympic contests. The Soviets were so good that they regularly thrashed an all-star collection of professionals from the North American National Hockey League.

Against this powerhouse, the United States sent its youngest Olympic team ever. Under the leadership of Coach Herb Brooks, the U.S. team worked hard and played an exhausting schedule of games. In pre-Olympic competition, they had performed well enough to be one of eight teams competing for Olympic medals. But any hope that the Soviets might stumble was doused when they

defeated Team USA, 10-3, in an exhibition game just a few days before the start of the Olympics.

As the United States struggled against Sweden in its first Olympic contest, it seemed the team would be lucky to earn any kind of medal at all. Sweden led 2-1 with less than half a minute to play. But then Team USA managed to salvage a tie on a long shot by Bill Baker.

In the next match, Czechoslovakia took an early lead. But the United States charged back to defeat the 1976 silver medalists, 7-3. Victories over Norway, Romania, and West Germany then sent the United States into the medal round of play along with the USSR, Finland, and Sweden. These teams would each play two more games, and medals would be awarded on the basis of each team's overall record for Olympic competition.

The joyride for Team USA was expected

53

U.S. goalie Jim Craig wards off a Czechoslovakian attack early in the Games.

to end abruptly in the first medal round, however. The early victories might have given the host-country fans a thrill, but now it was time for the United States to face reality. Skating out to meet them were the peerless Soviet Union players in their bright red uniforms.

In the first period, the Soviets seemed to be in control. Throughout the first 19 minutes of the game, the USSR outshot the USA, with 18 scoring attempts versus 7 for the United States. As the period came to a close, the Soviets led 2-1.

Then came the bizarre bounce that inspired the United States. With time running out in the first period, Dave Christian fired a long shot at the Soviet goal. Vladislav Tretiak, considered by many to be the finest goalie in the world, had only to sweep the shot to the side and his team would skate off the ice with the lead. But he let the shot bounce off him, straight to Mark Johnson. The U.S. forward rammed the puck past the startled Tretiak and into the goal to tie the game just before the buzzer sounded.

Irritated by Tretiak's lapse of concentration, the Soviet coach removed him from the game. It would hardly have mattered who they put in the nets during the second period, because the United States couldn't get near the Soviet goal. The Soviets peppered U.S. goalie Jim Craig with 12 shots during that period, yet the United States shot only twice. But despite their obvious superiority, the Soviets could score only once to take a 3-2 lead.

Between periods, Coach Brooks stressed to his players how close they were to achieving an incredible victory. As they had seen in the first period, a one-goal lead could be erased in a flash. In all their previous games, the well-conditioned United States team had dominated the final period. Brooks told his players that they were a team of destiny. If they played as well as they were capable of playing, something wonderful was bound to happen.

Team USA coach Herb Brooks inspired his young players at Lake Placid.

Wild jubilation accompanies the U.S. victory.

For the first eight minutes of the final period, nothing did happen. Then one of the Soviet players was penalized for an illegal defensive move. In hockey, minor penalties require that the offending player must sit out for two minutes without replacement. Mark Johnson used his team's one-man advantage to ram home his second goal of the game and tie the score. The home crowd thundered its approval, and chants of "USA! USA!" echoed off the walls of the arena.

Two minutes later, the chants grew even more deafening. Team USA's Mark Pavelich slipped a pass to team captain Mike Eruzione. Screened from the play by the whirling bodies in front of him, reserve goalie Vladimir Myshkin did not see the puck in time. Eruzione's blast shook the net for a goal. With only half a period left to play, the United States was actually leading!

For the next 10 minutes, the fans roared encouragement and cringed as the Soviets stormed the United States net. U.S. goalie Jim Craig was equal to the challenge, and his defensemen repeatedly helped by clearing the puck away from the attack zone. The crowd silently counted down the minutes. Then, as the frustrated Soviets were unable to mount a final assault, the fans noisily counted down the seconds. When they reached "zero," the building erupted in complete bedlam. A television announcer summed up the feeling as he shouted, "Do you believe in miracles?" Even the United States players, who were pounding each other in celebration, seemed totally shocked by what they had done.

After falling behind against the Finns in their final game, Team USA rallied to win in the third period. The miracle on ice was complete. Against all odds, the United States hockey team had taken the gold medal.

Eric Heiden stalks Yevgeni Kulikov in the men's 500 meters.

11

Hottest Thing on Ice

Eric Heiden
1980

Before 1980, Eric Heiden could walk just about anywhere in his home country, the United States, and not be recognized. At the same time, he could hardly make a move in Norway and the Netherlands without being followed by the press.

Heiden was a champion speed skater, a fact that impressed Europeans far more than it did Americans. But in 1980, the United States media was searching for possible heroes in the upcoming Winter Olympics to be held in Lake Placid, New York. When they discovered that Heiden had a good chance to win more individual gold medals than any person had ever won in a single Olympics, Eric's peaceful life was over.

The Madison, Wisconsin, native was not pleased with the change. All of a sudden, people were making tremendous demands on his time and were expecting him to win five gold medals. To do that he would have to win every skating race, from the shortest sprint to the longest endurance contest. He would have to outskate several world-record holders in their best events.

Heiden's reaction to the fuss over five gold medals was to ignore it. Whenever he was asked about his chances, Eric brushed off the question. He was not interested in a medal count; all he cared about was doing his best in the races and then going home.

As with Lydia Skoblikova's speed skating quest, Heiden started the competition with his weakest event, the 500 meters. The luck of the draw pitted him against the world-record holder in that event, Yevgeni Kulikov of the Soviet Union.

Kulikov churned off to a fast start, leaving Heiden a few strides behind.

broke the old Olympic mark by more than one second. None of the other racers came close to his time, and Heiden collected his first gold medal.

In the 5,000 meters, Tom-Erik Oxholm of Norway delivered a strong challenge, breaking the old Olympic record by more than 16 seconds in his heat! When Heiden's turn came, he seemed unable to match the Norwegian's relentless pace. Early in the race, his coach and teammates alerted Heiden that he was a full two seconds behind Oxholm's time.

Heiden didn't panic. With powerful, even strokes, the 21-year-old glided steadily around the track. Lap by lap, he began to chip into Oxholm's lead. With a strong finishing spurt, Eric crossed the finish line three seconds ahead of Oxholm's impressive time.

The gold medal, however, was not yet his. World-record holder Kai Arne Stenshjemmet of Norway had yet to race. While an edgy crowd looked on, the Norwegian stalked Heiden's time. With one lap to go, he was still close to Heiden's pace. Heiden's fans watched the clock anxiously as Stenshjemmet made his final push for the gold. True to his word, though, Eric did not seem

But after 100 meters (110 yds), Kulikov slipped while rounding a curve, and Heiden was able to catch up. The two skated evenly until they rounded the final curve. Then Heiden's massive, 27-inch (67-cm) thighs powered him past his rival as they streaked down the straightaway. Heiden's time of 38.03 seconds beat Kulikov by .34 seconds and

concerned. As Stenshjemmet glided across the finish line less than a second behind Heiden's time, the winner was off in the clubhouse, resting.

Gold medal number three came easily in comparison. Dressed in his bright gold bodysuit, Eric powered his way to victory in the 1,000 meters. His time of 1:15.18 smashed the Olympic record by over four seconds and gave him a comfortable 1.5-second win over Canada's Gaétan Boucher.

But the strain of three tiring races within a week began to show during the 1,500 meters. After starting strongly, Heiden slipped during a turn when his inside skate hit a rut in the ice. Another skater might have fallen, but the 185-pound (83-kg) Heiden kept control. After steadying himself with a hand on the ice, Heiden regained his rhythm. Again he broke the Olympic record—this time by nearly four seconds—and won easily.

The final race, the 10,000 meters, posed the biggest challenge. Again it was Tom-Erik Oxholm who applied the pressure. He completed his heat of the grueling 10,000 meters in 14:36.60, a full 15 seconds better than the Olympic record and just a second and a half off the world record.

After four tough races, would Eric have enough strength left to skate at a world-record pace in the longest race of all? A drained Heiden was not confident that he could do it. As a further

Tom-Erik Oxholm was a threat at Lake Placid.

Eric begins to pull away from Victor Leskin in the 10,000 meters. But could he hold his lead to the end of the grueling race?

challenge, the world-record holder in the event, Victor Leskin of the Soviet Union, had been paired with Heiden for this heat.

Early in the race, it appeared that Eric had no chance. He had barely covered 2,000 of the 10,000 meters when he began looking longingly at the lap cards. The fact that he was focusing on how many laps he had left, instead of concentrating on his form, was a sure sign that Heiden was struggling. But he steeled himself against the pain and exhaustion and began to pull away from Leskin. He was so tired that instead of leaning forward to maintain his momentum he was standing up in the turns to keep his balance. But he pressed on. By the final lap, Leskin was far back at the other end of the track.

Refusing to let up, Eric drove himself down the last straightaway, urged on by the enthusiastic crowd. He fought his way to the finish line in a time of 14:28.13, shattering the old world record by over six seconds! Somehow Eric Heiden had summoned the strength to make the last of his record five wins the best.

Before 1984, no ice dancers had received a perfect 6.0 score in Olympic competition. Jayne Torvill and Christopher Dean upset that tradition with their flawless performance at Sarajevo.

12

Performance Fit for a Queen

Torvill and Dean
1984

Throughout much of British history, the "common people" have been paying tribute to the royalty. In the 1984 Olympics, a pair of working-class skaters from Nottingham, England, turned that tradition around. Jayne Torvill and Christopher Dean were described in the English press as "Their Greatnesses." At the 1984 Winter Olympics in Sarajevo, Yugoslavia, Torvill and Dean put on such a brilliant exhibition of ice dancing that the queen of England wrote them a letter of appreciation.

Ice dancing, which is primarily a combination of ballroom dancing and ice skating, became part of the Olympics in 1976. At the 1976 and 1980 Olympics, the event was dominated by Soviet skaters.

The entrance of Dean and Torvill into ice dancing competition in the late 1970s put an end to both the rigid style and Soviet domination of the sport. Dean, a police trainee, and Torvill, an insurance clerk, began training in their hometown of Nottingham. As they improved, practices and competition began to take more time away from their jobs. To continue their ice dancing careers, they asked the Nottingham city council to provide money for their training. Although some believed it a scandalous misuse of public funds, in 1981 the council awarded £42,000 (over $65,000) to Dean and Torvill so they could train for the 1984 Olympics.

Three years later, no one in Nottingham begrudged having spent the money. Torvill and Dean had revolutionized the sport of ice dancing. Using a variety of creative dance steps, the two captured three consecutive World Championships prior to the 1984 Olympics. Their performances were so moving that many judges gave them perfect 6.0 scores.

Nineteen couples were skating in the ice dancing event at Sarajevo, Yugoslavia. But with the way Dean and Torvill were skating, everyone agreed that the only real competition would be for the silver and bronze medals. The 26-year-old Torvill and the 25-year-old Dean breezed through the compulsory

Natalia Bestemianova and Andrei Bukin of the Soviet Union

portions of the competition in which everyone skated identical dance steps and patterns. Then came the event that skating fans had been waiting for: the free-dance portion of the program. This four-minute routine would count for half of the final score. As in figure skating, a panel of judges rated the contestants on both technique and "artistic impression," or how well the routines conveyed the feeling of the music.

The Zetra Arena was packed, and the tension was building as the competition moved from the lowest-rated to the highest-rated dancers. Torvill and Dean were scheduled to be the last skaters. The Soviet couple that skated before them, Natalia Bestemianova and Andrei Bukin, excited the crowd with a spirited performance. Then it was time for the masters.

Torvill and Dean knew they could easily have won using traditional music and dance moves. But as Dean explained it, "Every year we try to do something different." This time they took a risk in choosing a very innovative theme for their performance—Ravel's *Bolero*, a slow-moving piece of music that people don't normally dance to.

The two started off on their knees, writhing and twisting in their flowing, purple costumes. Their slow-moving ballet told the sad story of a pair of lovers. Unable to live together, the couple swore eternal loyalty to each other and then hurled themselves into a volcano. Many of the judges were stubbornly in favor of traditional dances such as the waltz. Only a couple as talented as Torvill and Dean could have gotten away with such daring.

As the British pair skated their sensuous, emotional dance, the 8,500 fans rose to their feet, enthralled. When Torvill and Dean finished their performance, flat on the ice in a death pose, the crowd shouted their approval.

The judges also showed their approval. Three of the nine judges awarded them a perfect 6.0 score for technical merit (skating and dancing skill). The average of all the judges' scores in that area was a near-perfect 5.9.

Christopher Dean later commented that he thought that that day's performance had been more special than all the couple's other efforts.

The judges agreed. A second set of numbers flashed onto the scoreboard.

By the end of the performance, the dancers would lie flat on the ice. But the crowd in Zetra Arena would come to its feet.

These were the ratings for artistic interpretation. As the audience screamed in delight, the scoreboard flashed a series of nine 6.0s for the Nottingham couple! All the judges thought the performance was absolutely flawless.

Both the prime minister and the queen of England agreed and sent a note of congratulations to the pair. After viewing the performance of Torvill and Dean, they were willing to admit that, during the 1984 Olympics, Great Britain had a new royal couple.

Matti Nykänen shoots off the jumping ramp and soars aloft like a kite.

13

The Nuke and the Eagle

Matti Nykänen and Eddie Edwards
1988

Ski jumper Matti Nykänen soared through the air so lightly that it almost seemed as though he was rising higher into the air instead of gradually dropping to earth. Nykänen was considered by many to be the finest performer at the 1988 Winter Olympics in Calgary, Canada.

Ski jumper Eddie Edwards, on the other hand, looked more like a wounded duck plummeting to the ground. He was unanimously considered to be the worst athlete at the Games. Ironically, the fans and the press gave at least as much attention to the ungainly Edwards as they did to the graceful Nykänen.

Nykänen (pronounced NUKE-an-en) had been captivated by the thrill of ski jumping ever since he took a slide off the roof of his house at age seven. After the ninth grade, he dropped out of school to dedicate himself to the sport.

Averaging an incredible 6,000 jumps per year, most of them off his hometown hill at Jyväskylä, Finland, Matti became a world champion while still a teenager. He won the 90-meter jumping competition at the 1984 Winter Olympics by the largest margin in the history of the Games. At the same time, he made numerous enemies with his arrogant attitude and hot temper.

During the summer of 1987, Nykänen had two knee operations—something that would normally end a ski jumper's career. But by 1988, at the age of 24, a far more mature and polite Nykänen was back. He hoped to make Olympic history at Calgary by becoming the first jumper to win both the 90- and 70-meter jumps.

Eddie Edwards was the same age as Matti Nykänen, but that was the only similarity between them. "Eddie the

Eddie the Eagle was popular with the fans even though he finished last in each event he entered.

daredevil from Cheltenham, England, to be a refreshing change in the high-pressure world of international competition. He jumped so awkwardly, yet was so enthusiastic, that many of the other jumpers were charmed by his determination.

The only ones not captivated by Eddie the Eagle's courage were the Olympic officials. Some criticized Edwards as a disgrace to the sport of ski jumping. Others wanted him banned from competition for his own safety. But when the 70-meter competition began, Eddie took his turn alongside greats such as Nykänen.

No one could come close to "Matti Nukes" that day. Nykänen soared 89.5 meters (98 yds) on his first effort, the best jump of the two rounds.

On the second jump, Nykänen again sailed through the air for 89.5 meters and won the competition by a wide margin. Eddie the Eagle finished last with jumps of about 55 meters (60 yds).

Matti's quest for a second gold medal was delayed several times when the 90-meter jump was postponed because of high winds. The delay might have destroyed the Finn's concentration in

Eagle" held the British ski jumping record—but he was Great Britain's only ski jumper! Edwards had no financial backing and little training. All he had was a desire to compete.

Many competitors considered the

earlier years. But now he calmly waited for the winds to die down.

When the competition finally opened, Edwards was among the 55 competitors. With 52,000 fans looking on, Eddie the Eagle barreled down the chute. He wasn't in the air for long. Eddie again finished last in the competition by a wide margin, riding out a best leap of 72 meters (79 yds). Yet the fans cheered wildly for the courageous young man.

When Nykänen began his long descent from the tower, he could see the blue and white Finnish flags fluttering far below in the valley. Snapping into his takeoff, Nykänen soared high into the air. He floated and floated, longer than seemed humanly possible. When he finally landed, Matti had traveled an incredible 118.5 meters (130 yds), opening up a huge lead. He had come so close to reaching the foot of the hill that officials made all jumpers start from a lower point on the jumping ramp for the second round, just to be safe. In the next round, Nykänen added a 107-meter (187-yd) jump to his total to easily outdistance Erik Johnson of Norway.

Having made history by being the first to win both the 70- and 90-meter

The "Flying Finn" displays his three gold medals.

jumps, Nykänen went on to win a third gold medal in the team-jumping competition. As usual, Matti Nukes had the best jumps of the day. There was no team competition and no medal for Eddie the Eagle. Yet Eddie may have earned as solid a place in Olympic lore as Nykänen. Between them they gave a powerful demonstration of both the skill and the courage that have produced the Winter Olympics' greatest moments.

Read these other Sports Talk books by Nathan Aaseng:

Great SUMMER OLYMPIC Moments
Football's INCREDIBLE BULKS
Football's MOST CONTROVERSIAL CALLS
Football's MOST SHOCKING UPSETS
Baseball's GREATEST TEAMS
Baseball's WORST TEAMS
College Football's HOTTEST RIVALRIES
Pro Sports' GREATEST RIVALRIES
RECORD BREAKERS of Pro Sports
ULTRAMARATHONS: The World's Most Punishing Races

ACKNOWLEDGMENTS: Photographs are reproduced through the courtesy of: pp. 1, 2, 26, 29, 68, 71, Pressfoto; pp. 6, 8, 9, 10, 12, 16, 19, 20, 21, 22, 30, 32, 37, 38, 41, 42, 48, 50, 52, 54, 55, 56, 58, 60, 61, 62, 64, 66, 67, 70, Bettmann Archive; pp. 14, 15, Library of Congress; p. 18, National Ski Hall of Fame; pp. 24, 34, Italian Olympic Committee; pp. 44, 47, Kishimoto Corporation. Front cover: Pressfoto. Back cover: Focus on Sports.